MY JOURNEY TO HELL!

A Graphic Illustrated Experience

The True Life Experience of Dr. Michael H Yeager

Copyright © 2014 by Dr. Michael H. Yeager

www.docyeager.com

All rights reserved. No part of this book may be reproduced, stored in a retrieval system, or transmitted in any form or by any means-electronic, mechanical, photocopy, recording, or otherwise-without prior written permission of the copyright owner, except by a reviewer who wishes to quote brief passages in connection with a review for inclusion in a magazine, website, newspaper, podcast, or broadcast.

Unless otherwise indicated, all Scripture quotations are taken from the King James Version (KJV) of the Bible.

Acknowledgments:

I give praise & honor to Jesus Christ my Lord, Savior, & King, who without His divine intervention, I would not be sharing about my Journey to hell in this book, but I would literally be there.

To my one and only precious wife of 36 years, Kathleen Maye Yeager, who has faithfully labored with me in the harvest field all these years, even in the midst of much pain & sorrow.

To my precious five children, Michael, Daniel,(and his wife Yu) Steven, Stephanie and Naomi (who is now with the Lord).They all have worked at my side doing the will of God. May the Lord give them a rich reward. No father could ask for better children.

MY JOURNEY BEGINS

Now, one night I was deep in prayer with Willy, an African American brother in my barracks. I had the privilege of seeing Willie come back to Christ. At one time previously he had walked with the Lord but had backslid.

Before and after he was saved our nickname for him was "Willy Wine" because now he was filled with new wine. Now, as we were praying together, something very strange and very frightening began to happen to me. At the time of this event there was a gathering of some men in our battalion. They were having a party in the common area right outside our sleeping quarters where we were praying. The party they were having was quite loud with music and laughter, but it did not hinder us from crying out to God for souls.

As we were praying, I could sense that something was about to happen. The hair on the back of my arms and neck stood up on end. It was as if electricity was filling the very atmosphere around us. I sensed a strong tugging to go deeper in prayer. I gave myself completely over to the spirit of intercession, crying out to the Lord once again to experience the sorrows and agonies of hell. Please understand that I believe God put this desire, this prayer, into my heart for the love of souls. I began to pray in a realm that I had never been in before when suddenly an overwhelming and tangible darkness descended upon me.

"And when the sun was going down, a deep sleep fell upon Abram; and, lo, an horror of great darkness fell upon him" (Gen. 15:12).

A frightening darkness enveloped me. Everything around me disappeared. I no longer heard the music or the party that was taking place. Even though Willie was right there with me, I did not hear or see him. And it seemed as if time itself had come to a stop. Then too my utter shock, amazement, and horror, the floor and the building around me began to shake more violently than I had ever experienced before. Usually when we did get a quake it would only last a matter of seconds. But in this situation the shaking did not stop as it normally did, rather it increased.

All I could do at this moment was to try to hug the floor and hang on for dear life. The darkness lifted, but I could not see Willie anywhere. Then a terrible ripping and grinding noise filled the air. I saw the floor of the barracks ripple like that of a wave on the sea. The very floor of the barracks that I was laying upon began to tear and rip apart. I watched in stunned amazement and horror as the floor tiles popped and stretched. The concrete and steel within the building began to twist and rip apart. And the floor I was laying on began to split and tear open right below me.

I immediately began to look for a way to get out of the building. Everything was shaking so violently that I could not get up off the floor to make a dash to escape. The dust and dirt in the room was so thick and heavy that I could hardly breathe. Now this rip in the floor began to enlarge and became an opening. I would call it more like a hole. I began to slip and fall into this hole; I tried desperately to reach for any kind of handhold that I could find. I began to scream and yell for help. But there was no one to help me. I became more and more desperate trying to grab hold of something, anything that I could get my hands on. Objects around me began to fall through this hole in the floor. I watched as physical objects slipped past me into this hole. And I could feel myself sliding more and more.

No matter how desperately I was trying to cling to and hold on to items to prevent my falling, there was nothing that I could do. Finally, I slipped and fell backward as if falling off a ladder. As I was falling, everything seemed to go into slow motion like film that is slowed for a preview. I was falling with parts of the crumbling building all around me. I watched as I fell past twisted steel beams, concrete floors, walls ripped into pieces, plumbing and heating pipes, and sparking electric wires. I went past the underground tunnels that connected the buildings together.

The next thing that I knew I was falling past the ground and rock of the island. This terrible rip in the earth, this hole that I was falling down began to take on the form and similarity of that of a well, like an endless tube, an ever-proceeding pit. It became approximately three feet wide. As I was falling, I was desperately trying to grab hold of the rocks that were protruding from the sides of this deep dark pit, but my descent was too fast. None of the rocks seemed to protrude far enough for me to get a good handhold.

Even as I was falling down this hole I was not experiencing any fear of going to hell or fear of dying because I had a calm assurance that I knew my heart was right with God. I was ready to meet my Savior. Don't misunderstand; I am not saying that I had no fear! Though I knew in my heart that I was right with God, I was still filled with the absolute horror of not knowing what was happening to me.

At that moment I did not have any idea whatsoever that I was plunging into hell.

THIS IS TAKEN FROM MY BOOK CHRONICLES OF MICAH! BUT IT IS WHAT REALLY HAPPENED TO ME!

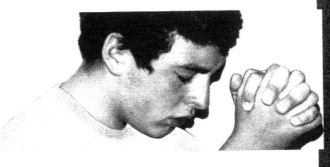

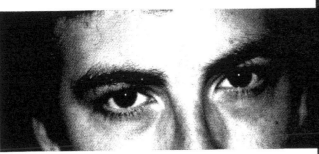

"Dear Lord, I want to reach out and touch those who do not know You. I know in my head that they are eternally lost and damned, but I need to see it; I need to experience it; I need to feel the agony of the damned. Oh, Father God, if I am to be consumed with a heart of true compassion, I need to know what awaits the lost. Let me experience the judgement of Hell, even as others."

Through the years Micah had experienced dreams, nightmares, and hallucinations from drugs, but none of them compared to what he was experiencing now. It was so real that Micah could feel, smell, and see everything.

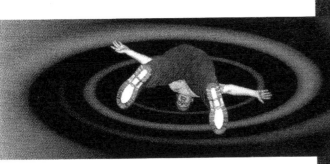

The sensations he experienced were beyond mortal description.

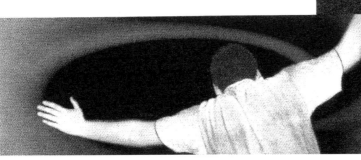

And then, Micah was out of the black hole.

He began falling like a sky diver at approximately twelve thousand feet above a gigantic lake.

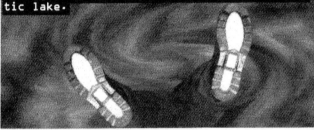

An ocean, burning, churning, bubbling!

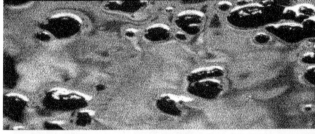

Boiling similar to a pan of molasses on a stove.

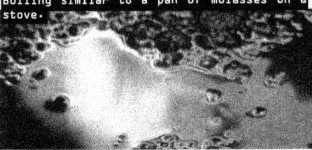

He could smell the sulfur, a nose-burning, sickening gas.

Fire and brimstone exploded, sending flames rising thousands of feet into the air. The flames darted here and there like a huge gasoline fire, only to vanish one moment then to appear the next moment somewhere else. The liquid was swirling like melted liquid tar, except it was not black. It glowed different colors of red, orange, and yellow. Perhaps a better description would be that it pulsated and radiated like hot charcoal in a furnace with molten steel, liquefied stone, and swirling gas dancing across the top of its surface like tornadoes — sea devils — until they ascended up into a black nothingness.

"What is that sound?" Micah asked himself.
His ears were filled with a strange, eerie
hum, like a throbbing
moan that never stopped.
As he fell closer and closer to the surface of
the firey liquid,
the moaning increased in intensity.
Louder and louder it grew.
The moaning sound became more distinct and
contained ear-piercing highs and incredible
heart-breaking lows with many
other pitches in between that were too numer-
ous to describe. "What can that be?" Micah
asked himself subconsciously.
At that very moment, it was like a fog
cleared from his mind. It hit him like an
old, Twentieth-century locomotive train
human beings!
The sound was coming from human beings who
were screaming from such intense pain,
unbelievable agony, and unbearable torment.
Micah's whole body began to shake violently
with shivers of absolute dismay and fear.

God had heard his prayer,
and God had, for some strange reason,
answered his request quite literally.
There was no turning back.
There was no stopping what had begun.
Micah was headed straight for Hell.

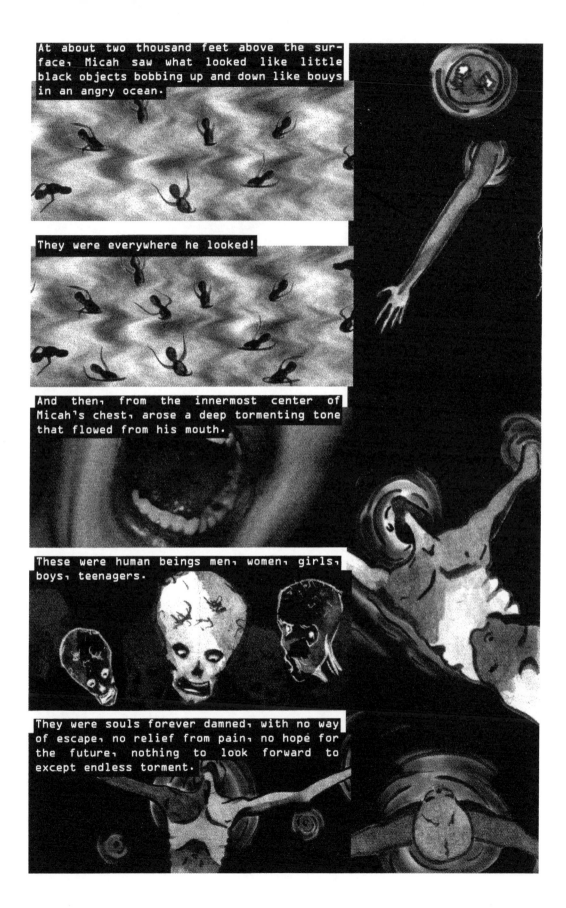

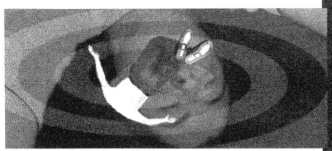

Because Micah was so caught up in the stark reality of what lay before him, he didn't realize that he was still falling closer to the surface of the bubbling, churning lake of fire, until he suddenly plunged into the lava.

It engulfed him — swallowed him up in its hideous mouth of endless suffering.

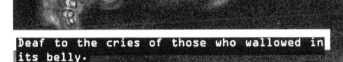

Deaf to the cries of those who wallowed in its belly.

It covered him over and filled his mouth, his nose, his ears, and his eyes with an intense burning, searing agony — Immersed in a baptism of absolute horror!

His eyes felt like they were being burned out of his sockets. His whole body was aflame and burning like a wick on the end of a candle.

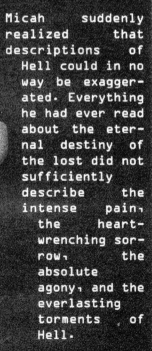

Micah suddenly realized that descriptions of Hell could in no way be exaggerated. Everything he had ever read about the eternal destiny of the lost did not sufficiently describe the intense pain, the heart-wrenching sorrow, the absolute agony, and the everlasting torments of Hell.

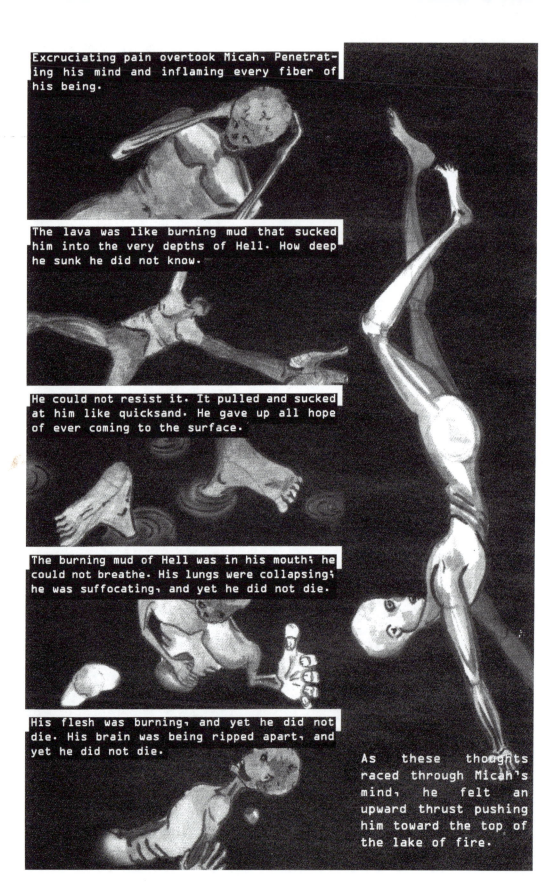

Excruciating pain overtook Micah, penetrating his mind and inflaming every fiber of his being.

The lava was like burning mud that sucked him into the very depths of Hell. How deep he sunk he did not know.

He could not resist it. It pulled and sucked at him like quicksand. He gave up all hope of ever coming to the surface.

The burning mud of Hell was in his mouth; he could not breathe. His lungs were collapsing; he was suffocating, and yet he did not die.

His flesh was burning, and yet he did not die. His brain was being ripped apart, and yet he did not die.

As these thoughts raced through Micah's mind, he felt an upward thrust pushing him toward the top of the lake of fire.

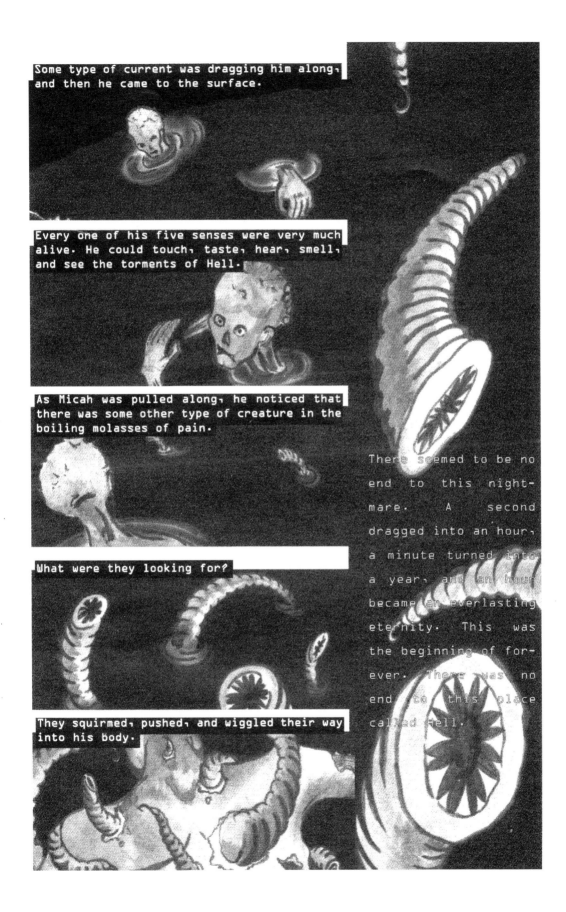

Some type of current was dragging him along, and then he came to the surface.

Every one of his five senses were very much alive. He could touch, taste, hear, smell, and see the torments of Hell.

As Micah was pulled along, he noticed that there was some other type of creature in the boiling molasses of pain.

What were they looking for?

They squirmed, pushed, and wiggled their way into his body.

There seemed to be no end to this nightmare. A second dragged into an hour, a minute turned into a year, and an hour became an everlasting eternity. This was the beginning of forever. There was no end to this place called Hell.

In the midst of the pain and agony,
another greater torment began to flood his soul.
It wasn't only one,
but multiple; it wasn't just physical,
but emotional.
Here, in this place called Hell,
there was no love.
It was a total void of love.

Micah exclaimed, "Even when I was a sinner, I was surrounded by the love of God!
A guardian angel from the Lord was always there
to protect me, even though I could not see him.
Nature, birds, animals, and all creation
displayed the unfathomable love of God.
The shining sun, green grass, budding flowers,
blue-gray waters of the sea,
light blue skies, and the sparkling stars at night all
professed God's awesome love for His creation.
The beautiful fragrances that floated on the wind, the
singing birds with beautiful songs, and many other
lovely, God-inspired gifts spoke of
His glorious creation.

But here, in this God-forsaken,
burning slime pit called Hell,
there is no love whatsoever."

A loneliness beyond description came upon Micah.
Even though he bumped into many others like himself,
there was no communication.

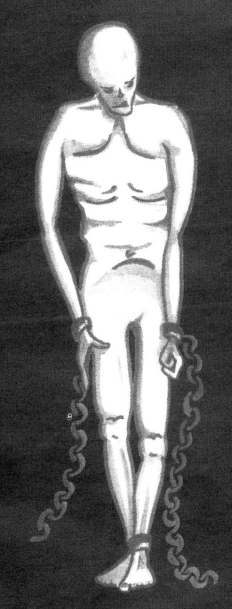

In Hell, there was no help, no relief, no escape, and no
hope. Forever and ever, there was nothing but torment.

A thirst gripped Micah, a thirst so intense, so maddening, he thought he would lose his mind.

If only he could have just one drop of water,

just enough to wet his lips.

But there was none to be had.

There was no relief, no freedom from pain.

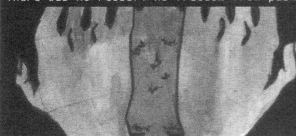

In Hell, the body does not go numb; the pain only continues.

"How long have I been here?" Micah questioned himself. He had been crying out in pain, unconsciously screaming like the rest of the damned. Yet his cries were of a totally different nature. Their cries were cursings, profanity, wickedness, and promises of repentence if given another chance, only to be followed by more curses. But Micah's cries were to God praising, and acknowledging that from God came his help. He proclaimed that God was righteous in His judgments, and that He was true and faithful and worthy of all glory and honor.

Then from somewhere within Micah, arose a scripture found in the book of Jonah. He thought about Jonah, when he was in the belly of the big fish, deep under the sea. A strong urge came upon Micah to pray these words to the Lord his God for his own situation, from within the depths of Hell.

Micah prayed, "I cried out of my pain and suffering to the Lord, and He heard me out of the belly of Hell I have cried, and You heard my voice. For You cast me into the deep, into the heart of Sheol, the abyss surrounded me, covering me. Then I said, I am cast out of Your presence and Your sight yet will I look again toward You. I went down to the bottom, to the very roots of the center, and the earth with its bars closed behind me forever. I found my place with the damned. Yet You have brought up my life from the pit and corruption. Oh Lord you are my God. When my soul fainted within me, I earnestly and wholeheartedly cried out to You. And my cry came unto You. Those who are around about me curse and blaspheme Your worthy name. But as for me, I will sacrifice to you with the voice of thanksgiving. Yet will I trust in You, Oh Lord, for salvation and deliverance belong to the Lord!"

And God said, "Let My servant Micah go."

The bowels of the lake of fire twisted and turned...

Then vomited Micah out.

The Rest of this Book Is Taken From My Book: The Horrors of Hell & The Splendors Of Heaven!

Out of Hell

At that very moment, it was almost like hell itself vomited me out. Incredibly it felt like I was being shot out of a canon. The next thing I knew, I was standing on the edge of a high and steep cliff. No longer was I in hell, but I was standing on the lip of a cliff looking straight down into the ocean of torment I had just been suffering in. The ocean of hell was still bubbling, boiling, and churning. And I could feel some of the heat of it hitting my body. The stench of it was still suffocating. I would say that the cliff was probably over a thousand feet high. As a looked around, I noticed that the land around me was virtually flat, with no vegetation. It all looked like it was compacted brownish, gray soil, with rocks and boulders. As I looked behind me there seemed to be a mountain range on the far horizon. As I looked to my right side, I noticed that in the distance there was what looked to be a wide, dark, slow-flowing river. It was pouring its contents like Niagara Falls over the edge of the cliff into the yawning mouth of hell.

But there was something very strange and eerie about this river. I did not want anything to do with this river. Actually there was this overwhelming desire in my heart to run as far away from it as I could. I knew that there was something very wrong about what I was seeing. In my heart I sensed that whatever the river was, it would bring to me tremendous pain and sorrow perhaps even more so than what I had experienced in the bottomless pit of hell. And yet, with this knowledge, this foreboding and dread in my heart, I knew that I must go to this river. The Spirit of God was prompting me to go and investigate. So instead of running away from this river, I found myself walking along the edge of the cliff, toward the river. As I got closer and closer, I began to tremble and shake. I could barely breathe. I had to take short gasps of breath. I could not believe, and I did not want to believe what I was seeing before my very eyes.

A Broad and Wide Road

This broad and wide, dark- river was not flowing with water, as I had supposed. It was made up of multitudes and multitudes of people, masses of humanity without number.

"Enter ye in at the strait gate: for wide is the gate, and broad is the way, that leadeth to destruction, and many there be which go in thereat" (Matt. 7:13).

I could see that there were those of all nations, tongues and peoples. I saw the dress of every religious group you could imagine. Upon this road there was a range of people who were both young and elderly. And by looking at their mannerisms and dress, you could determine to some extent what their livelihoods were. There were people of all professions—doctors, nurses, plumbers, professors, pastors, teachers, housewives, factory workers, policemen, farmers, milk men, bankers, military personnel, politicians, and world rulers.

"And he saith unto me, The waters which thou sawest, where the whore sitteth, are peoples, and multitudes, and nations, and tongues" (Rev. 17:15).

"Multitudes, multitudes in the valley of decision: for the day of the LORD is near in the valley of decision" (Joel 3:14).

As I drew nearer and nearer to this river, I could see that the people were walking on what looked to be a very wide asphalt road that made its winding way as far as my eyes could see into the horizon. Every inch of the road was packed to capacity with humanity, like sardines in a can. It seemed almost impossible for people to be packed so tight and so close together.

Now this road came right to the very edge of the cliff. At the cliff it broke off with jagged edges hanging over emptiness. It looked like a road would if an earthquake had transpired with the earth dropping out from underneath a major highway! And below this broken highway was the yawning, never-satisfied mouth of hell.

Headed to Destruction

    As I came closer to this river of humanity I found myself unconsciously looking deep into the faces of those who were walking on this broad and wide road. None of them, I literally mean that none of them seemed to be in the least bit concerned at all about where they were headed. They did not seem to be concerned about their future or where they were going. They did not seem to question the direction in which they were walking. Many were laughing and jesting. Others simply engrossed in conversation. Others caught up in their own problems. As I looked upon their faces I could perceive in my heart who they were and what they were going through. I knew in my heart that by the Spirit of God I was experiencing their sorrows, pains, loneliness, and depression. I also perceived the hopes, dreams, and visions that they had in their hearts, that which they had not yet apprehended or achieved. But not one of them seemed to be concerned about what was about to happen. Or where they were going. It was as if they were sleepwalking, like they were slumbering not realizing the danger that was just before them. It was as if they were blind to their eternal damnation.

"And the cares of this world, and the deceitfulness of riches, and the lusts of other things entering in, choke the word, and it becometh unfruitful" (Mark 4:19).

"And he spake a parable unto them, saying, The ground of a certain rich man brought forth plentifully: And he thought within himself, saying, What shall I do, because I have no room where to bestow my fruits? And he said, This will I do: I will pull down my barns, and build greater; and there will I bestow all my fruits and my goods. And I will say to my soul, Soul, thou hast much goods laid up for many years; take thine ease, eat, drink, and be merry. But God said unto him, Thou fool, this night thy soul shall be required of thee: then whose shall those things be, which thou hast provided? So is he that layeth up treasure for himself, and is not rich toward God" (Luke 12:16-21).

    At about twenty feet from the end of the road a small handful of them would seem to begin to wake up. At that moment it would become a totally different story. The reality of the situation seemed to finally dawn upon their faces. As they were pushed forward they began to try to push back against the oncoming masses. And the more they were pushed forward, the more frantic they became. They began to scream and cry and yell for help. But it was too late; they could not detach themselves from the masses. They were pushed forward, inch by inch, foot by foot. Those on the very edge of the cliff would seem to lose their mind in absolute terror as they saw more clearly what was awaiting them at the bottom of the cliff. It was as if their eyes were popping out of their head.

    Never have I seen faces so contorted with absolute horror and fear. I knew they could not believe what they were seeing. They began to push back with all of their might, clawing, hitting, scratching, trying to crawl over the top of those who were unwillingly pushing them to their destruction and damnation. Screams of unbelievable horror came from their lips as they would try to hang on.

Shouting and screaming with such deep desperation that it breaks my heart retelling it to you. It did not seem as if those who were only a few feet back could hear or see what was taking place until it was their turn. Or maybe they simply chose to ignore the commotion, because it did not yet involve them. They were so caught up in their daily living until destruction came upon them without warning.

"For when they shall say, Peace and safety; then sudden destruction cometh upon them, as travail upon a woman with child; and they shall not escape" (1 Thess. 5:3).

"But as the days of Noah were, so shall also the coming of the Son of man be. For as in the days that were before the flood they were eating and drinking, marrying and giving in marriage, until the day that Noah entered into the ark, And knew not until the flood came, and took them all away; so shall also the coming of the Son of man be" (Matt. 24:37-39).

Into the Abyss

As the people on the broad and wide asphalt road fell over the jagged edge, I watched them dig their fingernails into its unyielding surface. Not being able to hold on, they would continue to claw at the rough cliff walls, leaving trails of their precious human blood. The cliff wall was covered and matted with human blood, flesh, and bones. You could hear their pitiful screams for help as they tried to stop their descent into hell. As they plunged toward hell I would watch them spinning and tumbling head over heels. No horror flick ever made could express the absolute terror and horror I was watching take place before my eyes. These peoples' worst nightmares were coming to pass— nightmares that would last throughout eternity. When their bodies hit the burning, liquefied lava of hell it would create a splash like that of a rock dropping into a puddle of mud. For a few seconds I could see them struggling, still floating on the surface of the lake of lava, like a leaf on the water. Their clothes would catch on fire. Their hair would go up in flames and be consumed. Their identities were lost. No longer could you tell that they were male or female. Their nationalities, their ages, even the color of their skin was devoured in the burning torments of hell. Oh you cannot believe the terrible, heart-wrenching screams as they hit the surface and began to burn. They would slowly sink into the burning mud of hell, swallowed up in the never-ending undercurrents of this ocean of damnation. These were men and women, young and old, grandmas and grandpas, and teenagers. These were people of all nations and cultures from every diverse aspect of life. For hell is not a respecter of people.

My friends, please listen to me, hell is real. The Bible says that hell is:

- A great fire
- A fierce fire
- An irresistible fire
- A continual fire
- A dark fire
- An unquenchable fire
- An everlasting fire

Why People Are in Hell

People are in hell because of rebellion and disobedience to God. It is what the Bible calls sin. And what is sin? It is when you live by the standard of this: Not God's will be done, but my will be done. It is living a self-centered life, which is the gateway to hell.

It is the broad and wide path that leads men to eternal damnation, to separation from God where there is never-ending anguish, unutterable sorrows, everlasting pain, and eternal torments.

"Enter ye in at the strait gate: for wide is the gate, and broad is the way, that leadeth to destruction, and many there be which go in thereat" (Matt. 7:13).

Sin is being self-pleasing, self-loving, self-obsessed, self-centered, self-serving, and self-seeking. It is the vain pursuit of ungodly pleasures. Sin is rebellion and mutiny, and disobedience to God and His holy Word. It is that which is contrary to God's divine nature and His character, spitting in the very face of the One who died for us and gave Himself for us. Those in sin make themselves god, sitting upon the throne of their own heart with no pursuit of the Father's will. I beg you with all the sincerity of my heart, that if you do not know Jesus Christ in a personal, intimate way, please turn to Christ right now and come out of your sins. Turn from your self-pleasing and wicked ways. Please change your mind, and give Jesus your heart, soul, life, mind, and body. We need to give all of our selves to Jesus, even as He gave all of Himself for us! Jesus, by His own divine nature, will give you complete and total victory over the satanic nature.

"Whereby are given unto us exceeding great and precious promises: that by these ye might be partakers of the divine nature, having escaped the corruption that is in the world through lust" (2 Pet. 1:4).

You see God became a man and gave Himself as the ultimate sacrifice for our sins. Thereby providing the victory we need to overcome the world, flesh, and the devil.

"For this purpose the Son of God was manifested, that he might destroy the works of the devil" (1 John 3:8).

He died to save our souls and to resurrect and create His divine image and nature into our hearts once again. We must determine in our hearts to give Him all that we are, all that we have, and all that we will ever be. We have borne the image of the earthly fallen Adam. Now we must bear the image of the heavenly Adam. Beloved, are you walking on the broad and wide way of sin, which leads to eternal destruction? Or are you walking on the straight and narrow pathway of loving God, loving holiness, loving faith, and loving obedience?

"The wicked shall be turned into hell, and all the nations that forget God" (Ps. 9:17).

"The way of life is above to the wise, that he may depart from hell beneath" (Prov. 15:24).

You see, my friend, we will all someday die. It does not matter who you are or what you possess. You and I will die.

"For what is your life? It is even a vapour, that appeareth for a little time, and then vanisheth away" (James 4:14).

God's Heart Broken

As I watched these masses of humanity falling into the bottomless pit of hell I literally could not handle it. I ran from the edge of the cliff alongside this road of damned humanity like one who has lost his mind. I wanted to escape the sight of the pain and agony etched in peoples' faces as they were falling over the cliff. My heart felt like it was totally and mortally wounded. I felt like I was being stabbed with a huge knife that was slowly twisting and turning inside of me in my heart. My heart felt like it was being torn out of my chest. Now, if I felt this way, can you imagine how God feels? People believe that after Jesus suffered on the cross that He no longer suffers. But this is a sadly mistaken assumption. For the Father, Son, and the Holy Ghost are still in deep agony and pain over the fate of humanity. God's heart is broken over the loss of humanity and of the angelic realm that disobeyed and rebelled against Him.

"In all their affliction he was afflicted" (Isa. 63:9a).

"For we have not an high priest which cannot be touched with the feeling of our infirmities; but was in all points tempted like as we are, yet without sin" (Heb. 4:15).

But if God knew that this was going to be the end result, why would He create the angelic realm and humanity? For me to share with you the ultimate purpose and conclusion of God's plan would take a book within itself. I'll do the best I can with a quick explanation. Because God Himself is the giver, He wants to share all that He has with His creation. The only problem is that His creation cannot handle all that He has.

Lucifer is a major example

The little bit of glory, position, and power that God gave to this archangel ultimately became his downfall. Of course, Lucifer and the angels that followed him have no excuse. They knew in their hearts what they were doing was evil and wrong. That is why they are not given an opportunity for salvation. The moment they rebelled against God and sinned against heaven, they were eternally locked into their damnable natures. It would be like taking pure water and dumping black ink into it. You can never make it clear and clean again.

God wants to share His wealth, abundance, power, and glory that He was willing to pay the ultimate price to bring about a creation that would love Him. They would love Him to such an extent that no matter how He blessed them, they would not rise up against Him. He could cause them to become one with Him and yet be totally submitted in every area of their existence. It would have to be a creation that had already been tempted, tested, and tried. It would contain those who had experienced the evil of selfishness and rejected it in order to love their Creator. Beloved, this is what it's all about. We choose to love God more than ourselves or the pleasures of this present time. Therefore we are esteemed worthy of all that God is, has, or ever will be. According to the Scriptures we will rule and reign with Christ forever, simply because He first loved us. We rise up against the sinful nature that is in our flesh, which has penetrated our souls, following our beloved Savior and Shepherd wherever He may lead.

Sufferings of Christ

The suffering of Christ is still a great mystery to many of those in the church even. This suffering did not begin in the garden of Gethsemane. It literally began before the creation of all things. The Scriptures declared He was slain before the foundations of the world.

"And all that dwell upon the earth shall worship him, whose names are not written in the book of life of the Lamb slain from the foundation of the world" (Rev 13:8).

"But with the precious blood of Christ, as of a lamb without blemish and without spot: Who verily was foreordained before the foundation of the world, but was manifest in these last times for you" (1 Pet. 1:19-20).

From His birth to His resurrection **Jesus Christ** has suffered for you and me. In **Isaiah** chapter **53** it says **He was a man of sorrows and acquainted with grief**. It broke His heart to see the masses of humanity reject Him as their Messiah, for He knew that there was no other way than through Himself for men to be saved. We can only become partakers of the divine nature through the seed of **Christ** within the soil of our hearts.

It truly is all about Jesus. I would challenge every believer to buy a new Bible, and with a yellow highlighter, highlight every time it refers to **Jesus** in an intimate and personal way beginning in Matthew through the end of the book of Revelation. You would be amazed and shocked to discover that the Scriptures refer to **Jesus** approximately nine thousand times. That's over nine thousand times in approximately 163 pages.

As we see **Jesus** moving toward His ultimate sacrifice, His personal suffering increased. The night He was betrayed by Judas, He sweat great drops of blood (see **Luke 24:44**). He declared that His soul was close to death because of His suffering. All of the sins of humanity were being poured into Him. He never committed sin, but Scripture says that He was made sin that we might be made to be partakers of His righteousness. All of His suffering—the stripes upon His back, the crown of thorns upon His head, His beard being ripped out of His face, the spitting mocking and bruising of His body, dragging that rugged cross up Golgotha's hill— was for our salvation. When they threw His body down upon the tree and nailed His feet and hands to it with spikes, Christ, God in the flesh, allowed Himself to be brutalized and violated for our salvation. Even the heavenly Father had to turn His back upon His own son. Can you imagine how it broke the Father's heart for Him to have to turn His back on His only begotten Son?

"And about the ninth hour Jesus cried with a loud voice, saying, Eli, Eli, lama sabachthani? that is to say, My God, my God, why hast thou forsaken me?" (Matt. 27:46).

How could any human being not love Him? But that was not the end of His suffering. Scripture declares His soul descended into hell. This is very important for us to understand. His Spirit did not descend into hell, but it returned to the Father from which it came.

"And when Jesus had cried with a loud voice, he said, Father, into thy hands I commend my spirit: and having said thus, he gave up the spirit" (Luke 23:46).

"He seeing this before spake of the resurrection of Christ, that his soul was not left in hell, neither his flesh did see corruption.

This Jesus hath God raised up, whereof we all are witnesses" (Acts 2:31-32).

The reason why there is so much confusion in some of these areas of understanding is because we have not rightly discerned the Word of truth. Many years ago I discovered not to wrestle with the Word but simply to acknowledge, and believe, even if it contradicts everything I've ever been taught. I simply embrace the truth no matter where it leads. And then God gives me understanding within the context of those Scriptures. It is a wonderful and beautiful freedom. It is only when we allow the philosophy and indoctrination of naturally thinking men, which contradicts the teaching of God's Word, to influence our lives that we wrestle with the scriptures. This also gives the enemy of our soul, the devil, the right to blind our eyes from the truth.

The soul of Christ took the sins of humanity into the depths of hell to be left there forever. Jesus is able to help us because He knows the pains and sufferings of not only life but separation from the Father. He knows the torments of hell. Surely we can trust our eternal souls to such a loving Savior.

I Have to Do Something

I ran from the dreadful scene before my eyes. I ran until I could run no more. Out of breath I finally slowed to a walk. As I continued to walk, I realized that I must do something about these masses and masses of people that were headed straight to hell. I was still walking alongside this wide, broad, river of humanity but away from the cliff. So I began to shout to them, pleading and begging them to come off the road. I warned the people with all the compassion of my heart, with tears cascading down my face, flowing like a river, weeping, and pleading nonstop.

"Oh that my head were waters, and mine eyes a fountain of tears, that I might weep day and night for the slain of the daughter of my people!" (Jer. 9:1).

"Rivers of waters run down mine eyes, because they keep not thy law" (Ps. 119:136).

I tried everything I could, knowing that every minute that passed more and more people were falling over the cliff. And because I had experienced the pains and torments of hell I knew what they were about to experience and that they would never get out. I was preaching the thunder and the lightning of heaven. Then I would speak the love and mercy of the goodness of God. I preached the reality of Jesus and His atoning sacrificial work. With all the truths that I had available I declared God's kingdom that I might rescue some.

Would Not Listen

Many of these people on the road would stare at me as if I had lost my mind. Some would yell back at me, telling me to mind my own business. Some yelled that they were Christians, and that they were going to heaven. And others would seem to listen, with tears flowing down their cheeks. They would say that they wanted to come off of the broad and wide way, but they could not, that their hearts were too addicted to sin. They did not believe that Jesus had the power to deliver them, that they were beyond hope. Some said that they had blasphemed the Holy Ghost and therefore there was no salvation available for them. Others declared that they loved sin too much to let go of it. The demonic hordes were whispering in their ears, lying to them that God would not forgive them, that they were too far gone, or that hell was just a make-believe imaginary place.

"But if our gospel be hid, it is hid to them that are lost: In whom the god of this world hath blinded the minds of them which believe not, lest the light of the glorious gospel of Christ, who is the image of God, should shine unto them" (2 Cor. 4:3-4).

Laborers Few

I knew in my heart that the work before me was too great for one person alone. I desperately needed help to reach these this multitude of lost souls. One person by himself could not make barely a dent in evangelizing this ocean of humanity. I began searching to find someone, anyone, who could help me reach all these people.

Clusters of Saints

As I looked out across the flat plateaus, I could see clusters of objects in the distance. I could not make out what they were, but they seemed to be shining with a brilliant white. They were not on the broad and wide road but directly off to the side of it. As I moved farther up the road I saw that these white objects were in what appeared to be small and large groupings. And as I looked out over the plain, I noticed there were more of these clusters. Not just one or two but hundreds of them were scattered across the horizon. Some appeared to be extremely large and others were very small with many different sizes in between. As I drew closer to the first one, I discerned there was some type of movement taking place in these brilliant white clusters. As I drew closer it became apparent to me what they were.

These clusters were made up of people wearing glistening white robes. They were all grouped together in circles, facing inward, sometimes back to back. Their backs were to the river of humanity walking on the broad and wide road and to all else. The closer I came near these clusters, the more it became clear what was happening. Many of those within these clusters had their hands lifted up toward heaven. As I got closer I could see smiles of joy radiating from their faces. Tears were running down their cheeks. They were singing amazing and beautiful songs of love for Christ. At times one or more would break out in what seemed to be a prophetic Word.

From what I could hear, most of these songs were about how much God loved them and about the blessings that would overtake them in their walk with the Lord. These songs said that they were precious and important to Jesus and to the heavenly Father. I realized automatically who these people in white must be. They were fellow believers and saints in Christ—brothers and sisters in Jesus Christ. All of these clusters of saints seemed to be lost in their devotion to and for God.

But they seemed to be lost, totally and completely oblivious to the masses of humanity that were just a few feet away from them being led to an everlasting, never-ending, eternal damnation. They were enraptured in their own little spiritual experiences. They were enthralled with singing songs of praise and worship. There was no denying the sincerity; it was evident in their involvement and enthusiasm. But what good is sincerity, blessings, joyful spiritual experiences, and Holy Ghost parties if you are not concerned about anyone else except your own little group. It's what Scripture refers to as sounding brass and twinkling cymbals.

"Though I speak with the tongues of men and of angels, and have not charity, I am become as sounding brass, or a tinkling cymbal. And though I have the gift of prophecy, and understand all mysteries, and all knowledge; and though I have all faith, so that I could remove mountains, and have not charity, I am nothing. And though I bestow all my goods to feed the poor, and though I give my body to be burned, and have not charity, it profiteth me nothing" (1 Cor. 13:1-3).

A divine and supernatural urgency rose up in my heart. I tried to push my way into one of these clusters. And as I did I found myself yelling and pointing to the river of humanity. It was not anger, self-righteousness, or disgust that moved me but God's love. It was His overwhelming love and compassion that was being shed abroad in my heart by the Holy Ghost. It was love for the unconverted, lost, and blind sinners.

I desperately needed help to reach the lost masses upon the road of destruction. I knew in my heart that the heart of God was being broken because His people were not having compassion upon those who had not yet come to love and know Him, those who had not yet been converted and become new creatures in Christ Jesus.

Our Cross

When I was finally able to get one group's attention, they looked at me as one who looks upon a lunatic. "Look. Look," I said, pointing toward the broad and wide road. "Millions upon millions of men and women, young and old, are only a short distance from your cluster. And they are headed right for hell. We have got to do something. Please, please help me to reach them!"

The worship and praise stopped. No one in the group moved. It was like they were in a stupor. Since it seemed like I had their attention, I continued with my exhortation for them to help me reach the lost. Finally, one of the men spoke up. "Excuse me, brother, but God has not given us a spirit of condemnation. It seems to us that you are trying to bring us into bondage with this legalism. Whom the Son has set free is free indeed. You're putting this heavy guilt trip on us, and that definitely cannot be God. And to be quite blunt with you evangelism is not our ministry." For a moment I was totally dumbfounded. Surely this brother in Christ had to be joking. There is no way that anybody could be that ignorant of God's Word and God's heart. For a minute I was in such shock that I could not answer them. The Holy Spirit rose up within me, and out of my mouth came Scripture after Scripture.

"And Jesus said unto them, Come ye after me, and I will make you to become fishers of men" (Mark 1:17).

"For the Son of man is come to seek and to save that which was lost" (Luke 19:10).

I kept pleading and imploring them to help me pull humanity from the flames of hell. But no matter what I said, they did not seem to understand what I was saying. And I could not get them to move. I remember standing there completely frustrated, weeping, and crying uncontrollably. Not only for the damned but for those who called themselves believers.

Somehow the enemy of our souls has deceived the majority of the church into a place of spiritual complacency and pacifism. Now, there is no denying that there is some small measure of concern for the lost. But there's not the red-hot fervency and overwhelming love for souls that we should have. It is so sad that it seems that those within the body of Christ do not believe in hell themselves. God's number one concern is for souls to be saved.

"And he said to them all, If any man will come after me, let him deny himself, and take up his cross daily, and follow me" (Luke 9:23).

Soul winning is the cross that every believer is called of God to carry. God is calling every one of us to win souls. This is what the Scripture means when it says to love your neighbor as you love yourself.

"I have planted, Apollos watered; but God gave the increase. So then neither is he that planteth any thing, neither he that watereth; but God that giveth the increase. Now he that planteth and he that watereth are one: and every man shall receive his own reward according to his own labour. For we are labourers together with God: ye are God's husbandry, ye are God's building" (1 Cor. 3:6-9).

In the Harvest

I fell to my knees on the ground under tremendous sorrow and the heavy burden that was upon my heart, surrounded by these brothers and sisters in Christ. I closed my eyes as I wept with heavy sobs praying that God would open the eyes of humanity and of His church. I prayed that God would forgive me for my lack of concern and love. I prayed that the Lord of the harvest would raise up laborers for the harvest field. How long I prayed, I do not know. When I finally opened up my eyes, I found myself back in my barracks upon my knees weeping in prayer.

Willie Wine was on his knees right off to the side of me. I saw a strange expression on his face. Neither one of us said anything for a while. I noticed there was no music or sound of the men in the background. I asked him what was going on? He told me that they heard me screaming, crying, and wailing in the most unbelievable, heartrending and horrifying ways. He said they were all scared and ran for it. Willie asked me what had happened? During all the hours that I was experiencing this supernatural visitation from the Lord, Willie had been in prayer right at my side. I tried to describe to him everything that happened. Partly due to this visitation, a miniature revival took place on our military base.

From that moment forth an overwhelming burden came upon me. My love for Christ and souls went way beyond what I had experienced before. I became extremely desperate to reach souls for Christ, on the streets and highways, malls and shopping centers, Laundromats, and bar rooms. Wherever I could reach people, I was there.

HEAVEN IS GODS PLAN FOR YOU! WILL YOU CO-OPERATE?

About the Author

Dr. Michael H. Yeager is a pastor, author, motivated speaker who would love to come and minister to your church or group. You can reach him through the following:

Address:

Jesus is Lord Ministries International

3425 Chambersburg Rd.

Biglerville, Pennsylvania 17307

Phone: **1-800-555-4575**

Websites:

www.docyeager.org

www.wordbroadcast.org

www.hellsreal.com

www.jilmi.org

VISIT: Docyeager.com to access Pastor Mike's videos, books, latest meetings, and up to date news!

Made in the USA
San Bernardino, CA
28 May 2014